The Successful Bartender

Putting People Skills to Work

The Successful Bartender

Putting People Skills to Work

Geoff Colvin
Peter Battistella

Behavior Associates

Eugene, Oregon, USA

Interior Design: Kylee Colvin, Ahren Osterbrink
Interior Photos: Kylee Colvin, Getty Creative Images, Peter Battistella, Geoff Colvin
Cover Design: Kylee Colvin
Cover Photo: Kylee Colvin, Neville Colvin, Ahren Osterbrink
Editing: Celene Carillo, Mary Rosenbaum

ISBN 0-9631777-4-5

URL: http//www.behaviorassociates.org.

Printed in the United States of America.

Published and distributed by:

Behavior Associates
P.O. Box 5633
Eugene, OR 97405
USA

Tel: (541) 485-6450
Fax: (541) 344-9680

Behavior
Associates

Acknowledgements

The authors wish to acknowledge the following people who have made contributions to the content of this book and for participating in interviews: Lesley Battistella, Richard Becker, Gary Christopherson, Carl Cole, Peter Colvin, Zig Engelmann, Tiffany Esperago, Jerry Jaqua, Tim Keeley, Trudy Logan, Diney Mabbutt, Patty Madrid, Mike McCreery, Joe McCully, Pete O'Rourke, Dave Poppe, Mike Riley, Clayton Walker, Bryan Wickman, and Norm Zimmerman.

Thanks are due to Chris Coleman, owner of The Keg Tavern, Eugene, Oregon, U.S.A. and Leonie Hogarth, Licensee of the Golden Vine Hotel, Bendigo, Victoria, Australia, for permitting us to use their bar to take many of the photos in this book.

The Keg Tavern, Eugene, Oregon, USA

Golden Vine Hotel, Bendigo, Victoria, Australia

About the Authors

Geoff Colvin, PhD, has worked in the field of education for more than 40 years. He has specialized in dealing with serious problem behavior with students in schools. At the University of Oregon and in U.S. schools, he has spent many years researching how best to manage these troubled students and to train educators and teachers on how to manage them in the classrooms and schools. He has written more than 80 publications on how to teach and manage difficult children including a best seller, "Managing the Cycle of Acting-Out Behavior in the Classroom," and a Telly Award video program winner, "Defusing Anger and Aggression." He is presently a national educational and behavioral consultant.

Peter Battistella. Perhaps it was only by chance Peter became a hotel owner in Australia. Having completed high school in 1958 with Geoff, the first author, he became a civil engineer. But after many extended absences from his family, with five children, his wife suggested they look to buy a motel. After a couple of motel inspections their broker dropped a bombshell saying, "You are fun loving people. Do you really want to spend hours behind a reception desk to periodically hand over a room key & rarely see your customers again?" To which they replied it sounded a bit boring. They eventually bought the Cumberland Hotel in Castlemaine, Victoria, Australia, from whence they finally emerged after 18 years with a multitude of funny, unbelievable, and when one of their regulars died, sad stories. So, their broker was right. They were destined to be "hotel people." It is to the memory of all their customers- drinkers, diners, overnight & casual residents, that he dedicates his contributions to this book.

Author Team. These two authors, high school buddies, have combined their career experiences to write this practical book on people skills for bartenders. Geoff brings to the table his vast experience from working with problem behavior and is able to provide information on understanding the problems and describing effective solutions. Peter, with his own professional background, coupled with almost 20 years actively owning and working in a bar, has a solid understanding of the bar scene. His contributions help to ensure the material presented in this book is grounded and workable for bartenders.

Contents

Introduction

Successful bartenders today have to be skilled and knowledgeable in a wide variety of ways. They must know hygiene rules governing public drinking places; know how to mix all the various kinds of drinks that may be ordered; manage the till and money efficiently; have the necessary people skills to meet individual and group needs to maintain reasonable service and order; know the laws for excessive drinking and under-age drinking; manage large crowds of customers; solve problems when they arise; keep the tables and drinking areas clean; deal with customer concerns and complaints; manage additional services as necessary, such as the gambling areas and menus from the kitchen; work as part of a team with other staff members and many other responsibilities and expectations such as being interrupted to provide directions to some place; and knowing the latest news, gossip and sport results.

Multi-tasking is a very popular word in the work place today, which means that a successful worker needs to be able to manage many tasks *at the same time*. Well, there is no question that once we see all the things that bartenders need to do, *multi-tasking* is a key to their success.

Though bartenders need training in all of these areas of responsibility, this book addresses one particular area- *people skills and preventing problem behavior*. Some have said that successful bartenders have one thing in common- they have great tact in dealing with people. While some bartenders are naturals, others need to work at it to learn these essential people skills.

Bartenders have a unique job. One reason is that they have to deal with the same group of people on a daily or regular basis, as well as others who come in just occasionally or for a one-time visit. It is the repetition of constantly working with mostly the same group of people, some of whom are very pleasant while others may be quite difficult at times, that set bartenders apart. Many other professions such as tradesman, medical workers, and business people do not have this level of regular contact. Granted they all have to have people skills in their work, but they usually do not have the day-in and day-out contact with much the same group of customers that makes bartending especially challenging.

Another challenging aspect of being a bartender is that they have to become very good at "one way listening." This means that the customers often expect the bartender to listen to all of their woes and so-called accomplishments. But they have no interest in what the bartender has to share and they don't particularly care if the bartender is sick or injured. There is an expectation with many customers, that the bartender is there for them and that it is a one way street.

Also, another challenge in the bar business is that bartenders need to be very careful about announcing good news such as their "upcoming holiday in Hawaii," or their "purchase of a new car." The reason is that some customers resent bartenders spending money that they believe came from them. They sometimes think that they are overcharged for drinks, which is confirmed, in their eyes, when the bartender speaks of planned expenditures.

Dealing with these kinds of challenges are all part of people skills. If the bartender has poor people skills, these regular customers may get frustrated and find another place to go. Problems in the area of people skills can result in loss of income for the owner and probably loss of a job for the bartender. However, with good people skills neither of these results need occur. Bartenders must meet the challenge of developing good people skills to keep the regulars content and be able to nip problems in the bud if they occur. In this way, if the customers are satisfied, the bartender will enjoy the job more, and more income will be generated, making it win-win for all.

A key understanding for the bartender is to realize that alcohol consumption can change some customers' behavior and cause them to lose self-control and judgment. These customers may start out quite relaxed and having a good time. But, after a few drinks, their moods may change and they can become argumentative and insulting. Others may begin to flirt or make advances that are offensive. In other cases, the customer may fall asleep and need to be woken and asked to head home. With others, more serious problems may arise, such as the customer becoming threatening, throwing things around, brawling, and even becoming violent and unsafe. No one wants these incidents. People can get hurt, and the customers are there for a relaxed time and do not want these kinds of scenes. If these situations happen very often, then the clientele in the bar will change. The regulars may go somewhere else and more "rowdies" will be drawn to this bar. The bartender needs to learn how to defuse the situations when problems arise some customers drink more alcohol.

 ## Quotable Quote

If you want to understand what makes some businesses work and some fail, it's a simple interaction like this: someone willing to make a customer feel important.

~Trudy Logan, Restaurant Owner~

Some bartenders are very comfortable in a bar and people skills come quite naturally to them. Others have to work at it or never really learn these skills on the job. We believe that all bartenders can learn to use good people skills that make the bar a safe and enjoyable place for the customers, and that help the bartender become more successful and have a satisfying and rewarding job or career.

Having a relaxed drink in the bar

This book opens with Chapter 1, in which several scenes in a bar are desribed to illustrate how bartenders' people skills come into play. The idea is to demonstrate the importance of people skills in the bar and to give the reader a sense of what this book is about. Chapter 2 provides information to help the bartender understand the effects of alcohol on the behavior of customers in a bar. These changes in customer behavior are described in terms of levels, with the lower levels showing acceptable behavior and the upper levels showing increasing problems. The idea is that if bartenders can recognize changes in customer behavior, they will be in a stronger position to use the guidelines described in the following chapters. In Chapter 3, information is presented on how to keep the bar atmosphere relaxed and calm. Chapter 4 describes changes in the customer behavior that can pose problems. Guidelines are listed for the bartender to nip these problems in the bud. Chapter 5 addresses the worst case scenario, andthat is how to deal with the serious behavior that may erupt such as fighting and brawling. Chapter 6 presents information and strategies on working with a large group of customers coming into the bar, such as a local football team coming in after a big win. In the final chapter, Chapter 7, the main ideas in the book are drawn together and followed by some concluding remarks.

While this book is written primarily as a tool for bartenders, it should also prove to be useful for personnel who work directly in or around bars such as security, waitresses and waiters, and table cleaners. Moreover, the information should be very valuable to owners and managers who have the responsibility to train and supervise staff. It is also expected that the information could be used with initial training and licensing for bartenders and for on-going training.

The authors are well aware that there are many differences from one bar to the next. Some bars are located in high-end restaurants, while others are found in rough neighborhoods. There are also differences in standards of behavior tolerated in bars. For example, in one bar foul language is not tolerated at all, whereas in another bar language is not an issue. In one bar, altercations and fighting may be fairly common, yet in another bar these conflicts are never seen. Some bars serve food, which becomes part of the bartender's work. In some bars bartenders stay behind the bar at all times, whereas in other bars they are expected to bus tables and wait on customers. Also, some bars have a dress code and others do not. However, regardless of the variety found in bars, the authors maintain that good people skills are an essential tool for bartenders in *every bar*. It is up to bartenders to learn the norms, practices and culture of an individual bar, and adapt the general people skills described in this book to their situations.

Bullseye

End of game

1

Seeing People Skills at Work in the Bar

People skills are a highly valued tool for employees in most, if not all, service professions. How do people skills apply to bars? In this chapter, several examples of the use of people skills are described. The main idea of these examples is to convey to the bartender the importance of using good people skills in the bar and also to show what problems can arise when poor people skills are used.

Situation 1: Connecting with the Customers

Travis has been a bartender for years. As soon as customers come into the bar, he sees them, and gives them a wave or greeting. He moves to serve them as quickly as possible and says he is pleased to see them. He chats with them for a few seconds, and at the same time is looking around the bar to see if someone else needs attention. He gets their drinks and asks if there is anything else they need.

Comment: Travis has the people skills touch down very well. He sees newcomers, greets them, makes them welcome, serves them in a timely manner, and, at the same time, keeps a good eye on the rest of the bar providing quality service to all customers.

Situation 2: Disgruntled Regulars

Bill, Mary, Joe, and Lou come into the bar almost daily after work. They sit in a corner of the bar, have their drinks and chat away. Once they have several drinks, they begin to talk much more loudly and laugh a lot. The bartender is busy serving customers at the bar and getting some pizza going for other customers. Bill tries to catch the bartender's attention for another round of drinks, but she fails to acknowledge him, being totally immersed with the customers near her. He then shouts very loudly, "What does it take to get a drink here?" The bartender looks flustered and tries to finish what she is doing. Eventually, she goes to end of the bar and asks Bill what he needs. By this time, he is frustrated. He gruffly orders a round and does not say anything when the drinks arrive. This regular customer clearly communicates to the bartender that he is not pleased with the service.

Comment: Here is a case where some regular customers become upset because they are not served in a timely manner. There is no big scene or anything, just that the customers become a little disgruntled. Yet the bartender feels she is going flat out to serve everyone and will get to this group as soon as she can. In these cases, the bartender must always be looking around even when she is busy. In this way, she could have seen Bill trying to catch her attention and could have responded immediately with a remark, "I'll get to you very quickly" or make a signal that says, "Be with you in a minute." When she does get to them, she could have apologized for the delay with a remark like this, "Sorry to keep you waiting. It is getting so darned busy in here. What can I get you?" Most customers are reasonable and would be fine with this response from the bartender. Also, we must be aware that the customers' patience is usually lessened after they have had a few drinks, which makes it more important for the bartender to be looking around and keeping an eye on things.

Quotable Quote

I hate it when I am standing at the bar waiting to order a beer and the bartender is yakking on a darn cell phone.

~Dave Poppe, Customer~

Situation 3: The Very Quick Blow-Up

One customer was leaving the bar, and another one was sitting at the corner of the bar near the exit, having a few drinks. The customer sitting at the bar happened to be dating the ex-wife of the customer leaving. The customer sitting with a smirk on his face, winked at the one leaving. The customer leaving stopped dead and then lunged at him, pushing him back into the bar, and got into his face muttering a string of expletives. The bartender noticed the altercation and came over very quickly saying, "Mike, Bill, come on now, cool it or take it outside. This is not OK." The bartender stood there, holding his ground and waiting. The aggressive one left muttering something, and the other one said to the bartender, "I don't know what's up with him, I never said anything." The bartender said. "I don't know, but we can't have that kind of stuff happening here," and went back to the bar.

Comment: In this case the bartender may not have known the agenda between these two customers but was able to respond quickly, in a tactful and direct way, and defuse what could easily have developed into a brawl. The bartender did not take sides, the problem was prevented and both customers could return to the bar on another day. However, if the bartender was not looking around and keeping an eye on things, this incident might not have been noticed, and a fight probably would have happened.

Situation 4: Managing Volatile Situations in a Large Crowd

Saturday evenings in summer can be challenging nights for the staff at Dave's Bar and Disco. The reason is that there are usually very large crowds and the bar does not close until 3:00 am. Security staff has been hired for this part of the season. One particular night a customer started yelling and pushing people around him. The two security staff moved quite quickly to the customer, stood near him but not in an over-bearing way, and asked him to leave. The customer refused. The security staff held their ground, pointed to the door and moved either side of the customer (but again not too close). The customer, paused, muttered some expletives, and started heading to the exit. The security staff followed at a reasonable distance. Outside the door the customer attempted to shove one of the security staff who deflected the push. Both security staff moved close to the customer maintaining a defensive position and told the customer that he needs to leave the premises immediately or the police will be called and a complaint filed for disruptive behavior and attempted assault. One security person pulled out a cell phone. The customer cussed some more and then left.

Comment: This situation could have developed into a very nasty scene were it not for the management skills of the security staff. These staff members were able to take control of the situation in a calm and measured manner. They were not overly aggressive and yet were firm and decisive. They did not escalate the offending customer and most importantly they did not lose their cool when the customer tried to push one of them. They applied sound defensive measures and made it very clear that the bottom line of calling in the police would occur if he didn't leave the property immediately.

There is no question that these situations are very challenging to manage as the combination of a large crowd, loud music, access to alcohol and late hours can make for volatile situations. This incident highlights the importance of the need for careful training of security staff in managing large crowds of people, keeping a close eye on the crowd, defusing volatile situations, keeping their cool and having clear procedures when emergencies arise. Information on these topics is provided later in the book.

Disco night out

· · · · · · · ONLY IN THE BARS · · · · · · · · ·

NOTICE TO CUSTOMERS
All those who are drinking to forget, please pay in advance.
~The Management~

Situation 5: The Build-Up to a Serious Incident

Phil is pretty much a regular. This Saturday afternoon, he is in the bar visiting with some of his friends and having a few drinks. He plays a couple of games of pool and has a few more drinks. He seems to be relaxed and enjoying himself. Two hours later, they finish playing pool and head back to the bar to watch the football game on TV.

Meanwhile, after a few more drinks, they are chatting quite animatedly about the game, and the bartender notices they have become very loud. Phil, in a fairly serious way, says that this team will win the championship. Joe bursts out laughing and says that this team couldn't beat a team of ten-year olds. Now the whole group laughs. Phil thumps the bar and shouts, "You idiots wouldn't know what a good football team is!" The group goes quiet and pulls away. Meanwhile, Phil remains at the bar, continues to drink, and watches the game by himself. He finishes his beer and puts a $10 beside his empty glass and continues to watch the game. The bartender serves Phil another drink, makes a comment about the game as Phil mumbles and just stares at the TV. Shortly afterward, the bartender serves a drink to someone else and gives Phil his change. Phil looks hard at the change and says, "Where's the rest of it?" The bartender says, "What's that Phil? You gave me a ten." Phil says, "That's (expletive) I gave you a (expletive) twenty!" The bartender opens the till and shows Phil the ten dollar note on top. Phil says that was someone else's, scowls, and turns away to watch the game.

The game ends with Phil's team losing a close one. The bartender serves Phil another beer and is very careful not to say anything about the game, recognizing Phil's frustration. At this point, a newcomer takes a seat beside Phil, orders a beer, and makes the comment that the best team won. Now Phil stands up, slams down his drink, and glares at the stranger. The bartender moves quickly to Phil and says, "Phil, come on now. Take it easy." Phil backhands his glass knocking it on the floor, and storms out of the bar shouting a stream of expletives.

Note: This scenario could have ended in even uglier ways, such as a fight between the two customers, or with Phil throwing chairs and glasses around, or with other customers joining in resulting in a big brawl and police having to be called.

Comments: It is not hard to imagine what would have been different if the bartender had been keeping an eye on this development and used some tact or people skills, earlier in this scene. For example, when the bartender heard the conversation becoming loud, he or she could move directly over to the table and ask if anyone wanted anything. Or say to Phil, "Anything you need Phil?" and wipe the tables, straighten chairs, and maintain some presence in the group. In this manner the bartender is communicating in a non-verbal way: "We may be getting a little out of hand here and we need things to settle down." It is likely that Phil would have backed off at this point and the following events described previously would not have occurred. The idea is for the bartender to provide a distraction, shift the focus, break up the altercation and try to have the customers resume a normal visit to the bar. If the situation did worsen, then the bartender would need to be more direct, get their attention and say something like, "Listen fellas, we have to settle down. OK? We don't want any problems."

Situation 6: The Simmering Customer

A difficult customer to deal with is the one who simmers or just sits stewing over something. These are the guys who can explode unexpectedly. In this scene we have Carl, who has been sitting at the bar drinking quietly for a couple of hours. He is not engaging in conversation with anyone and has no change in his expression. A couple of others come in who know Carl and make some comments. The bartender noticed that Carl seemed to bristle when these two came in and he heard Carl mumble, "That's (expletives)," to something one of them said. The other two laughed quite loudly at Carl's remarks.

World Strongest Man (Well sort of …)

World Strongest Woman…?

Carl glared at them, muttered something under his breath, and headed off to the restroom. He came back looking quite mad and came up behind one of the two customers who was apparently bothering him and shoved the customer in the back, knocking glasses over and spilling beer on the table and floor. A major brawl followed, and police had to be called.

Comment: If the bartender was keeping an eye on things, it would have been clear that Carl was stewing over something. The bartender could have approached Carl and said something to him, just as a friendly greeting. No need to engage Carl (he wouldn't want that anyway), but just touch base with him. The bartender should have noticed that there was hostility between Carl and the other two. The bartender could have moved over to them and interacted a little. Perhaps it would have been a good idea to approach Carl privately and say something like, "I hope those guys are not getting to you, Carl. Should we call it a day?" Or, "Can you leave it alone?" or "Seriously Carl, it is not worth having a scene over this is it?" The idea is to catch it early and for the bartender to let Carl know that he or she knows things are brewing and doesn't want it to go any further. Also, the bartender is communicating that he or she is looking out for Carl and the other two customers. Moreover, if Carl has already attacked other customers on previous occasions, he should be asked to leave and not return for the sake of the rest of the customers.

People-Skills Focus of This Book

The focus in this book is to provide bartenders with strategies for keeping the bulk of the customers relaxed and satisfied. There is a strong emphasis on good service and respectful interactions. In addition, guidelines are described for defusing situations in the bar that could result in a serious incident. In other words, if bartenders can learn to recognize the signs of beginning problems and take sensible steps early, then big blow-ups or major incidents will be a rarity. Finally, suggestions are presented for dealing with these very rare situations when violence and unsafe behavior occur.

The basic approach in this book is to understand that blow-ups, brawls, and ugly outbursts of anger and violence are generally the result of a series of events and the on-going consumption of alcohol. These events usually start out quite small, but as time progresses and more alcohol has been consumed, the exchanges between customers can become more annoying, making the customers angrier. It is possible for the situation to develop into something serious and unsafe. This book is about describing people skills, or tact, that help the bartender notice these developments and step in a timely and tactful manner to nip the situation in the bud and prevent further problems.

People skills and good service are keys to maintaining a calm, relaxed, and comfortable bar and for preventing problems from escalating. This book is written to describe these skills for bartenders.

Quotable Quote

I love bartenders who accommodate you. You want more chairs, they get them for you. In fact they know you want more chairs before you even ask. You want separate tabs, they do it for you. The good bartenders are flexible and often anticipate what you need.

~Tim Keeley, Customer~

"Later. Thanks for coming in."

2

Understanding How Customer Behavior Can Change

In this chapter we provide ideas to help the bartender understand how customer behavior can change in a bar. In the vast majority of cases the customers' behavior is acceptable. They come into the bar for a few drinks, visit with their friends, have a quiet read of the paper or watch a game on TV. The bartender has an important role in using good, friendly service to make these visits as pleasant and relaxed as possible for the customers. In this way customers leave the bar satisfied and are likely to return; income is brought into the bar; bartenders become more fulfilled with their work; and job security is increased.

However, there are times when customers may push the envelope. That is, their behavior can change and become unruly, hostile, offensive, aggressive, and even violent or dangerous. The bartender is expected to be able to manage these customers, try to maintain peace in the bar, settle down the customer who may become disruptive and remove the ones who are too disruptive and unsafe. This can be a tall order for a bartender, especially if the serious behavior comes out of the blue. The bartender may not be sure what to do and could take action that only worsens the situation.

The purpose of this chapter is to assist the bartender in understanding how customer behavior can change in a bar from being calm and relaxed to becoming hostile and dangerous. If bartenders can understand what is happening, or about to happen, then they are in a good position to take action and prevent things from getting out of hand.

The Effects of Alcohol

First and foremost, the bartender must understand that continued consumption of alcohol can cause problems with some customers. In some cases there are escalations in behavior (where the behavior gets worse), and a loss of self-control and judgment. See Box 2.1.

Box 2.1: The Relationship Between Continued Drinking and Behavior

1. The customer's behavior can escalate following several drinks. Escalation means a steady or sudden worsening of behavior. Customers may start out fairly calm and relaxed, and as more drinks are consumed, they can become loud with talk and laughter. Some may go further in using profanities, getting argumentative and hostile, while others may go further still and want to fight and become violent. These escalations in behavior can occur as a result of continued drinking.

2. The customers begin to lose self-control and good judgment. This means the loss of physical control, which affects walking, coordination, speech, balance and above-all driving. In addition the customer's judgment may become impaired. The customers may begin to brag, and tell exaggerated stories. Quite often they cannot tell if they have had too much to drink, and they believe they are fully capable of driving. They become offended and angry when they are told they cannot be served more drinks, or that they shouldn't be driving.

Other factors can also contribute to these changes in behavior in the bar, such as a customer using drugs. Drugs and alcohol do not mix and drug users can become serious problems after they have had a few drinks. Other customers may come into the bar with weighty problems already on their minds, such as being laid off work, family issues or being angry with an individual customer because of some longstanding conflict. These customers can easily escalate after they have had a few drinks. Another factor is how long the customer has been in the bar. Occasionally, a customer may be in the bar from opening to closing or for a greater part of opening time. These customers obviously have the opportunity to drink a lot of alcohol, and problems can follow. Also, bartenders have noted that certain customers escalate when they switch to stronger drinks.

More Alcohol for Some Customers Can Lead to More Problems

A key point in dealing with customers in the bar is to understand the relationship between continued drinking and its effect on behavior. The basic message is that with some customers: The more drinks these customers have, the more chance problems will happen. This relationship is described in the following diagram, Diagram 2.1: Link Between Alcohol Consumption and Problem Behavior.

The centerpiece of the diagram is a glass which shows three levels of alcohol consumption and the corresponding customer behavior. The lowest level of alcohol consumption, low, shows a corresponding behavior as acceptable. The next level of consumption, medium, indicates behavior in the beginning problems stage. The highest level of alcohol consumption, high, has a corresponding behavior of serious problems.

Diagram 2.1: Link Between Alcohol Consumption and Problem Behavior.

The line on the left side of the diagram shows increasing amounts of alcohol being consumed, from low, to medium to high. On the other side of the diagram, the line shows increasing problems with behavior from acceptable, to beginning problems, to serious problems. In addition, the line indicating increasing problems is divided into a scale of 1-10 called the Problem Behavior Scale.

Scale for Levels of Behavior

For the purposes for discussion in the next chapters, we have added a scale, 1- 10 for the level of behavior displayed by the customer (Problem Behavior Scale). This scale means that at the low end (level 1), the customers are quite calm and relaxed. With a few more drinks, some customers may become rowdy and loud, but are still behaving in an acceptable range (level 4). Around level 5, the customers' behavior changes from being acceptable to showing signs of problems, beginning problems. In some cases, this can be a slow change, while with others it can be very fast. The customers may become argumentative around levels 5 and 6, and then become more angry and hostile at levels 7 and 8. The top levels, levels 9 and 10, refer to customers who exhibit very serious, violent behavior, such as fighting or trying to do bodily harm.

One of the biggest advantages of thinking about levels of behavior is that it helps the bartender determine where a customer is on a scale of one through ten, which in turn tells the bartender how to respond to this customer. For example, after several drinks the bartender might conclude that, "Sarah is at a number 5." This means that the bartender may need to keep an eye on Sarah. Or, if the bartender thinks a customer is at level seven or eight, then the bartender may conclude that the customer has reached his or her limit and needs to be refused further service of alcohol. The diagram can also help with communication between staff presently working and between staff who may be changing shifts. For example when Eloise takes over at 9:00 p.m. from Marty, Marty tells her that the group in the corner is at a number 4, and so it goes.

The main point with this diagram is that once bartenders keep an eye on their customers, they can tell which level of behavior they are showing acceptable, beginning problems or serious problems, and then use the appropriate people skills for keeping the customers at a tolerable level or for defusing a situation. Or, if unfortunately on those rare occasions the person becomes violent and safety becomes a big concern, then there are very definite emergency procedures for the bartender to follow.

Spread of Customers by their Behavior

Another very important concept in this book is that by and large the vast majority of customer behavior falls in the acceptable range (Levels 1-4). Some or very few customers show behavior that would be in the beginning problems range and very few indeed, rarely behavior that would be called a serious problem. This spread of customer behavior that a bartender might typically experience is represented by the following diagram, Diagram 2.2: Spread of Customer Behavior.

Diagram 2.2: Spread of Customer Behavior

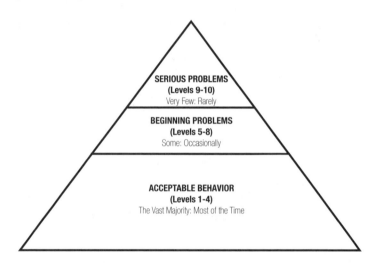

SERIOUS PROBLEMS
(Levels 9-10)
Very Few: Rarely

BEGINNING PROBLEMS
(Levels 5-8)
Some: Occasionally

ACCEPTABLE BEHAVIOR
(Levels 1-4)
The Vast Majority: Most of the Time

· · · · · · · **ONLY IN THE BARS** · · · · · · · ·

A duck waddles into a bar and orders three drinks. The bartender says, "That'll be $6.50 please." The duck says, "Put in on my bill, please."

Quotable Quote

Some guys come in and start out OK, but after a few drinks they flip personalities. Then you have to keep an eye on them.

~Patty Madrid, Bartender~

A fun night out

Illustration of Progression of Problems with Continued Drinking

The three photos on the following page show two customers who progress through the levels of behavior beginning with the acceptable levels, moving to beginning problems and finishing with serious problems resulting in the bartender having to tell them to leave. The first picture shows them having a relaxed conversation and toasting each other. Here they are in the acceptable range, Levels 1-2. After further drinking and visiting, they get into an argument, start shouting and finger pointing at each other, and making threats. The bartender asks them to tone it down a little. Here they have progressed further up the scale and are in the beginning problems range (Levels 5-7). Finally, after further drinking, they become physical and start to push each other, stand up and grab each other. Here they have now entered the highest levels, serious problems, Levels 8-9. While they did not get into an actual fight, the signs were there that a fight would have erupted, so the bartender told them to leave.

Photo Illustration of Behavior Worsening with Continued Drinking

Acceptable (Levels 1-2): Making a toast

Beginning Problems (Levels 5-7): Making threats

Serious Problems (Levels 8-9): Getting physical. Time to leave.

Chapter Summary

The main idea presented in this chapter, which is very simple, is that in the case of some customers, the more alcohol consumed, the more likely problem behaviors might be seen. The following table shows the links between these items of more alcohol and more problem behavior for these customers.

Amount of Alcohol Consumed	Kind of Behavior	Level on Scale 1-10
Low	Acceptable	Levels 1-4
Medium	Beginning Problems	Levels 5-8
High	Serious Problems	Levels 9-10

In the following chapters, 3 through 6, effective strategies or guidelines are described for managing the levels of behavior shown by customers from low levels through to the highest levels.

Four steps are used to describe the guidelines in each of these chapters:

1. **Main aim statement**, which captures the purpose of the strategies to be used,
2. **What you see**, in which the details are described for what bartenders may observe to help them determine which level of behavior the customers may be showing,
3. **What you do**, in which specific strategies are recommended to be used for the level of behavior observed with the customers,
4. **A summary** of the main strategies for the levels of behavior.

The basic diagram, Diagram 2.1: Link between Alcohol Consumption and Problem Behavior, will be presented with each chapter to serve as a pinpoint for the levels of behavior being addressed. The glass is filled to the levels being addressed in the chapter.

Acceptable higher levels (3-4)

3

Keeping Behavior Acceptable

Diagram 3.1: Acceptable Behavior, Levels 1-4

As you can see in the diagram (3.1: Acceptable Behavior, Levels 1-4), the customers' level of behavior stays in the acceptable range of 1 through 4 and does not rise above level 4 (see shaded area 1-4). This means that their behavior never really becomes a problem. Some customers may never rise above levels 1 and 2. They come in to have their drinks, enjoy themselves, leave, and return again. Others may reach levels 3 or 4 after more drinks and become rowdy and noisier, but they do not become aggressive or offensive. They too leave and return another time.

Main Aim: Levels 1-4
The Bartender Keeps The Customers' Behavior At The Acceptable Levels

It is most important that bartenders take every step to keep the atmosphere in the bar at the calm and acceptable level. When customers enjoy their visit, they are likely to return. This is win-win for everyone. Quite often customers have to meet with someone for one reason or another. If they are comfortable in a particular bar, then they are more likely to return to this bar for a relaxed visit or meeting. Moreover, if the bartender is active with efficient service and good people skills, there will be far less chance of problems arising.

ONLY IN THE BARS

A man goes to a bar with his dog and asks for a drink. The bartender says "Sorry. You can't bring dogs in here!" The guy says "This is my seeing-eye dog." The bartender says, "No, I don't think so. They don't have Chihuahuas as seeing-eye dogs." The guy replies "What?!?! They gave me a Chihuahua?!?"

Acceptable Levels 1-2

A relaxed chat.

Can you believe it?

Acceptable Levels 3-4

How about that?

Looks like we are having a good time here.

What You See
Acceptable Behavior: Levels 1-4

Clearly, acceptable behavior, the lowest levels 1-4, is what bar owners, bartenders and customers want in the bar. Customers typically come to a bar to relax, have a few quiet drinks, visit with friends, read the paper or watch some sports on TV, play pool, darts, and perhaps the gambling games. Here is a list of behaviors we might see customers showing at the Acceptable levels (1-2 then 3-4).

Quotable Quote

You know, customers don't want good service; they *expect it*. If they don't get good service, they will go somewhere else.

~Gary Christopherson, Market Owner~

Acceptable: Levels 1 through 2

This is the lowest level of behavior and clearly the most pleasant. These behaviors are usually seen during the first few drinks.

- Sitting quietly either alone or with friends
- Quiet conversation
- Body language is calm and comfortable
- Language is pleasant and acceptable
- Friendly banter and teasing is occurring
- Competitive exchanges in a friendly manner
- Some laughter
- Customers listening to each others talk or stories
- Other signs you might see

Acceptable: Levels 3 through 4

Many customers leave after a few drinks and do not really get to these next levels of behavior. Others may stay on and have several more drinks. The bartender may now see some changes in behavior that are still tolerable. These behaviors are:

- Noise level rises noticeably
- Conversation is louder
- Laughter is louder
- Customers interrupt each other more
- Some may get clumsier and knock over glasses
- More shouting across the bar is noticed
- More language or profanities are heard
- Other signs you might notice

· · · · · · · ONLY IN THE BARS · · · · · · · · ·

I walked into a bar the other day and ordered a double. The bartender disappeared and came back with a guy who looked just like me.

What You Do: Levels 1-4
Strategies for Keeping Customer Behavior at Acceptable Levels

The following guidelines are recommendations for bartenders to use with the aim of keeping the customers' behavior at the acceptable levels.

Look Around and Be Observant

Bartenders need to be looking around all the time. They must notice who comes in, who leaves, who needs something or if there is something wrong somewhere. Regardless of what bartenders are doing, they need to frequently look around the entire bar. They must be observant all the time and be ready to anticipate problem behavior at any time.

By contrast, bartenders who are intent on reading newspapers, watching TV, constantly washing and polishing glasses or engaging in long conversations with individual customers are not in a position to notice what is happening in the bar or see what is needed until it is too late.

The guidelines in this book are pointless if the bartender does not notice what is going on. Good timing requires that the bartender be aware and to be observant. See Box 3.1 for an illustration of one bartender being observant and another one not being observant.

Box 3.1: Illustration of Bartenders Being Observant and Not Observant	
Bartender Being Observant	**Bartender Not Being Observant**
Sarah is pulling three beers and she notices that two customers enter the bar. She nods to them, finishes serving the drinks, and says to the newcomers, "Be with you in a minute." She delivers the three drinks, picks up some empty glasses on the bar and asks the group at the end of the bar if they need anything. They want another round. She takes the order from the newcomers, serves them and hears a loud noise in the corner. She takes a step closer to see what is happening. She sees a chair is accidentally knocked over. She then gets the round for the group at the end of the bar.	Mike is busily pouring three drinks and has his eyes glued on what he is doing. He does not see the two newcomers enter the bar. He takes the three drinks to customers at the bar. He does not notice a signal from the group at the other end of the bar, with one of them saying, "Another round, please." Nor does he see the number of empty glasses on the bar. Mike then begins wiping the bar in front of him as the two newcomers seat themselves towards the end of of the bar and wait for service. Eventually one of them gets tired of waiting and shouts out to order a couple of drinks. The group at the end of the bar shout out that they need another round. Mike looks up confused and wonders why they are yelling at him. He hears the loud bang in the corner and heads over there. Meanwhile one of the newcomers from the end of the bar heads to Mike to ask again for their drinks, and both look annoyed.

Comments: It is not a hard question to ask which bartender was doing a better job. Sarah was in touch touch with the bar by looking around, being observant, and keeping in touch with the customers. Mike, on the other hand, had his head buried and did not notice the customers coming in, nor hear the order from the group at the end of the bar. Because he was not in touch, the customers were not getting served in a timely manner, even after they were shouting their order. So then they had to go to Mike directly to order. With Sarah, the customers were relaxed and taken care of. With Mike, the customers became frustrated because they were ignored and had to become aggressive to get Mike's attention.

Quotable Quote

A good football player takes in the whole field. A good bartender takes in the whole bar.

~Norm Zimmerman, Customer~

Be Welcoming

First and foremost when customers enter a bar they need to feel welcome. The bartender should notice them coming in and greet them as soon as possible. Use their names and make it your business to learn their names. One way of remembering names is to use the customer's name each time you serve the person.

As well as using the customer's name, it is helpful to add a welcoming short statement such as, "Hi Bert, good to see you," or "Hello Myrna and Mary, thanks for dropping in," or "Howdy Ted. How's it going?"

Serve Customers Promptly

Customers do not like to wait too long for service. Serve them as soon as you can, especially their first order. If you happen to be held up, for example, putting together a large round of drinks, let the new arrivals know you will be with them shortly. When you do get to serve them, apologize for the delay, "Sorry to hold you up –had a couple of big orders. What can I get you?"

Some customers like the bartender to know what they drink. However, it is recommended to always check: "Lite beer Norm?" In this way you are showing you know the customer and at the same time checking in case he or she may want something else.

Serve Customers in Order

Try at all times to serve customers in order. Some customers will get upset if others are served before them. This strategy is even more important once the customers have had a few drinks.

Unfortunately, even though bartenders may want to serve the customers in order, they will occasionally serve someone out of order just through human error. This may trigger customers to another level of behavior, especially if they have already had several drinks, leading to profanities or insults. Here the bartender must remain calm and try to defuse the situation with a remark like, "Hey Mark, take it easy, I'll get to you," or "Hey Mark, give me a break. I can't remember everything, you know."

Keep Contact With Customers

It is very important to keep contact with the customers so their needs can be met more swiftly. It also helps the bartender to spot any problems that may arise. The bartender should move up and down the bar or around the bar as much as possible by wiping down tables, picking up glasses, removing used dishes, pushing chairs into tables when customers have left, and checking to see if anyone needs anything. It is also important to talk to the customers while gathering glasses and cleaning. A very useful strategy is to ask the customers for permission to clean up around them to show them respect, especially when the cleaning up involves reaching in front of the customers.

Bartenders should be careful not to interrupt conversations too abruptly or barge in with something to say. Rather, they should politely ask if anything is needed. It is usually not a good idea to join in the conversations, especially in groups, unless you are invited. It is different if there is only one or two in the bar and you know them reasonably well.

Keep the Bar Clean and Orderly

The bar should be clean at all times. Customers will not return if the bar is dirty or smelly. The bar staff, while continually serving, needs to be constantly picking up, wiping down tables, emptying ashtrays, removing used dishes and glasses, picking up any trash on the floor and keeping passages clear as much as possible. Move quickly to clean up spillages. Check the restrooms or toilets periodically to see that they are clean. Customers expect the place to be clean. Just seeing the bartender frequently wiping down tables and counters tells the customer that this staff prides itself on having a clean bar. A clean bar is necessary for customers to feel comfortable and enjoy themselves. There needs to be a careful balance between cleaning and talking to customers. The bartender must be able to do both. In addition, some areas have laws governing the cleanliness of bars and violations could result in loss of license or fines for the owner.

Anticipate Orders

Customers appreciate a bartender who checks to see if orders are needed. This saves the customer from having to wait, make signals or shout across the bar. Customers often get irritated when they have to wait too long or have difficulty catching the bartender's attention. Bartenders who move around and look around can tell when customers are ready to order. It is also more efficient, when possible, to get orders from the group at one time versus coming back and doing each one separately. Otherwise, the bartender will be taking extra time going back and forth to this group, which can be a problem when the bar is busy.

Bid Farewell to Departing Customers

Just as it is very important to greet customers, it is also important to say goodbye to them. The bartender should notice when people are leaving and acknowledge them with a simple comment and use their names if you know them, such as, "Later Joann. Thanks for coming by" or, "Bye guys. Drop in again when you can," or simply just wave to them.

This is just another way of telling customers that they are appreciated. Moreover, if they are first-time customers, then there is more chance they will return.

• • • • • • ONLY IN THE BARS • • • • • • • •

A man goes into a bar and the bartender says, "What'll it be buddy?" The man says, "Set me up with seven whiskey shots and make them doubles." The bartender does this and watches him slug one down after another until all seven are gone. In disbelief, the bartender asks him why he's drinking so fast. "You'd drink them this fast too if you had what I have," he says. The bartender asks, "And what do you have pal?" The man says, "I have one dollar."

Summary of Strategies

The strategies recommended for bartenders to follow in creating and keeping a relaxed atmosphere in the bar are summarized in Box 3.1.

Box 3.1:Keeping Customer Behavior Acceptable
People Skill Guidelines for Bartenders
1. Look around and be observant at all times 2. Greet customers on arrival 3. Serve customers promptly 4. Try to serve customers in order 5. Make regular contact with customers 6. Constantly clean all areas of the bar 7. Know when customers need to order ahead of time 8. Bid goodbyes to all customers

Chapter Summary

The key to running a successful bar is having a place where the customers feel relaxed and comfortable. The bartender plays a very important role in establishing this kind of atmosphere by using people skills that help the customers feel welcome and valued. These people skills come down to two main guidelines in helping to keep customers at these low levels of acceptable behaviors:

1. Provide timely service.

2. Be positive and welcoming to all customers.

If bartenders become skilled at each of these two steps, then there is every chance that customers will remain in the acceptable behavior range and less chance of problems happening.

Quotable Quote

I tell my bartenders that their most important thing to do is BE AWARE.

~Mike McCreery, Pub Owner~

4

Anticipating and Defusing Beginning Problems

Diagram 4.1: Beginning Problems, Levels 5-8

Diagram 4.1: Beginning Problems, Levels 5-8, shows a rise in levels of behavior as the customer drinks more alcohol (note the glass is shaded to the beginning problem level range of 5-8). These customers may start out quite calm, relaxed and behaving in the acceptable range. However, after a few more drinks, and depending on their personal agenda or personality, customers may change and become angry and hostile. These customers show the signs of beginning problems. These changes may be slow and easy to see. On other occasions, the changes may be more sudden or blurred.

It is important to note that most customers at this level do not go further and get into fights or more violent behavior. These customers have learned to pull the plug at this level or they may have been burned in the past and do not wish to be axed from the bar or charged by the police. However, a very few will proceed further and the bartender may not be ready for this to happen. So it is important to anticipate these situations early by observing customer behavior and alcohol consumption, and prevent the possibility of more serious behavior happening.

Main Aim: Levels 5-8
The Bartender Anticipates Problems Early And Defuses Them

Even though the bartender may be doing a great job with using the people skills to keep things relaxed and customers' behavior at acceptable levels, problems can arise. The reason is that customers may bring agendas to the bar from home, work, or someplace else. Also, certain customers may be holding grudges against somebody else, and it doesn't take much for this hostility to show. So once the customer has several drinks, these hostilities may emerge.

The key in this chapter is for the bartender to catch the first signs of hostility and use good people skills to defuse the problem, so that it doesn't go any further.

Beginning Problems in the Bar

Loud arguing

Customer sleeping

Customers now standing making threats

What You See
Beginning Problems: Levels 5-8

Given the bartender is frequently looking around the bar, the first step is to recognize any signs of beginning trouble, such as signs of tension building up or customers starting to turn on each other. Bartenders must know what to look for. The clearest signs of trouble are changes in the customer's behavior. For example, an area of the bar may suddenly become quieter or noisier, or there are sudden movements in an area, such as people standing up, or outbursts of shouting and profanities. The beginning problems range of behavior is 5 through 8. Levels 5 through 6 have more to do with the customer starting to lose it or the beginning signs of anger. Levels 7 through 8 involve the customer becoming verbally aggressive and turning on someone, and becoming more hostile.

Levels 5 through 6

- Body language showing increased fidgeting, more movement, finger tapping
- Eyes dart here and there
- Excessive flirting
- Conversation becomes louder
- More gruffness appears or less polite interactions occur
- Strong reaction to teasing
- Language has more of an edge to it
- Bragging
- More tensing up and agitation can be seen
- Individual signs (the bartender may learn what individual customers do when they are getting angry)
- Other signs you may notice

Levels 7 through 8

At this point the customer is beginning to focus more on other individuals and does things that are highly likely to engage them in a challenging way. The common signs here are:

- Arguing
- Shouting at others
- Name calling, insults, and put downs
- Swearing or using profanities directed at someone
- Sexual advances

- Challenging remarks
- Excessive bragging
- Body posturing (leaning into the person, finger pointing, and squaring up)
- Threatening
- Competitive in a nasty manner (leaving the other no room to move)
- Comes across as combative
- Falling asleep
- Individual signs (the bartender may learn what individual customers do when they are becoming hostile)
- Other signs you may notice

What You Do: Levels 5-8
Strategies for Defusing Beginning Problems

Once bartenders see customers becoming tense, getting angry and perhaps hostile, it is very important that they act quickly to prevent problems from worsening. These people skills are called *defusing strategies*. The key in this section is for bartenders to anticipate any signs of trouble and take action accordingly. The prevailing strategy is to anticipate trouble and nip it in the bud.

Be Alert, Look Around and Keep on the Move

Once again, the first step is for the bartender to be observant. Clearly, if bartenders see what is going on then they can act quickly and defuse the situation. If they do not see the developments, then it will be too late to do anything to prevent a serious incident. Bartenders should also move around as much as possible in order to more easily hear what is going on and be in a position to act swiftly as needed.

Respond Immediately

Once the bartender notices tension arising, it is most important to respond as quickly as possible. This does not call for drama like rushing over and interrupting. Rather, it calls for a calm and measured response. Bartenders need to withdraw from what they are presently doing and move deliberately towards the problem area and engage in some normal activities such as wiping down tables in the area, and collecting glasses or used items. Sometimes just the presence of the bartender near the trouble spot can be enough to interrupt an altercation or a problem in the making.

The bartender can also ask if anything is needed being careful not to be abrupt. Rather just a quiet, "Need anything here?" or, "Are we all set here?" Another strategy is to chat a little to another person nearby who is not involved. The overall strategy is to let the customers, who may be tensing up, know that you are present

Be Calm and Respectful

It is very important for the bartender to be calm and respectful when problems arise. The main reason is that the customers may be beginning to lose it a little, and the calmness of the bartender helps to put things in perspective. The calmness and control shown by the bartender lessens the chance of the customers turning on the bartender.

In addition, other customers see how calmly and maturely the bartender handles the situation, which in turn helps set a nice tone in the bar, and the customers gain confidence in their bartender.

Don't Let Customers Take over the Bar

Sometimes regulars will try, in their own ways, to take over the bar. For example, a couple of customers might start bad mouthing an individual in the corner and urging the bartender not to serve him or her. Or some customers may be watching a game on the TV and some regulars tell the bartender to switch the channel to another game. It is important for bartenders not to yield to these pressures. The bartender is in charge and must not let certain regulars or locals take over. Everyone has a right to be served in the bar unless they lose that right by something they do versus what others may say. Also, if customers are already watching a game or listening to some music then they have the right for it to continue unless they are willing to make the switch.

Run Interference

This is an old strategy in which a slight distraction is used when a problem arises. For example, if two customers are beginning to get loud, the bartender approaches and says to one of them (given you know him), "Ted, excuse me a second. Are you playing this weekend?" Or simpler distractions could be to ask him or her, "Are you done with these glasses?" or, "Can I get you something else?" and stand there for a second or two. These minor distractions can help to defuse the situation simply by breaking up the focus between the customers.

Know What Certain Individuals Do When They get Confrontational

These prior signs of confrontation are general. However, certain individuals, whom we might call hot-heads, usually do much the same things when they are starting to lose it. For example, a sharp bartender will say, "Oh yes, Billy starts to get pretty mouthy and loose with the language. Then look out after that," or, "Jack starts to brag about when he was a star for the local football team," (many regulars knowing that Jack was a reserve most of the time). Others may begin to cross a line with flirting or making offensive sexual remarks or advances. It is important to know what certain customers do when they might be showing signs of losing control. This information will enable to bartender to act and defuse the situation before things get out of hand.

Use a Signal for Individual Customers

In some cases when an individual customer is beginning to lose it, it is helpful to have a signal or cue. For example, Wally starts to shout out foul language after he has had a few. On one occasion he went to another bar, The Rose, and began to shout foul language. The bartender told him that foul language is not permitted in The Rose. Wally continued to use the foul language and was told to leave. When he returned to his original bar and began to use foul language, all the bartender had to say was, "Hey Wally, 'The Rose,'" and Wally would stop using bad language. In this case, "The Rose" served as a signal to calm down and stop the language.

Defusing Confrontation between Customers

Once the bartender notices that some customers are getting confrontational with each other, it is very important to approach them and defuse the situation. For example, if two customers are shouting at each other the bartender should move towards them, stand firmly and say something like, "Everything OK here?" or "Do you need anything?" Then the bartender waits for an answer. It is always helpful to use their names if known. If the situation continues the bartender should be more direct but still polite and firm with a statement like, "Look, I hope this doesn't get out of hand, I don't want any trouble on my shift," or, "Listen fellas, we don't want any trouble here, let's cool it OK?" and stand there with the expectation that they will back off.

If the confrontation continues and they do not settle down, the bartender can tell them it needs to stop or they will have to leave. "Look if you can't settle down I will have to ask you to leave." If they do settle down, the bartender can thank them and ask if there is anything they need. If not, the bartender must follow through and ask them to leave.

Using a Straight-Forward Direction

In some cases a straight-forward and no-nonsense direction can be effective in causing customers to stop their behavior. For example, if a customer is starting to be offensive with profanities or sexual talk, the bartender might approach this person discreetly and as privately as possible say something like, "Hey Bill, knock it off OK," or, "Listen, take it easy would you? This needs to stop."

Watch out for Stirrers or Provokers

Sometimes there are customers who play a rule of being a stirrer. That is, they sense a conflict between other customers who are known, and begin to make comments that worsen the situation. This is more common if they don't like one of the involved customers. For example, a customer may be insulted by someone and the stirrer says, "Did you hear what he said to you?" or, "Are you going to let him get away with that?" Unfortunately, this stirring behavior is a way of life for some people. They seem to automatically become troublemakers when there is any opportunity.

Bartenders should move fairly quickly to these provokers and make their presence very clear with a question like, "Anything you need here?" and hover for a minute or two in their presence by cleaning the table, straightening chairs. If these customers are getting too involved, the bartender should ask them to back off with a comment like, "OK fellas, let's leave it alone eh," or, "We need to cool it here. OK." If they persist with this behavior they should be asked to leave.

Note: Several owners and bartenders reported in our interviews that they believe strong action must be taken with stirrers because they can quickly incite more serious problems.

Dealing with Personal Attacks on the Bartender

While some customers may get confrontational towards each other, others may confront bartenders, such as by shouting at them for an order or insulting them and getting in their face. In these situations, it is most important to avoid overreacting by arguing back or worse still, returning an insult. Once the bartender reacts like this, things can easily get worse. Bartenders must understand that when customers insult them they want you to react or buy in. It really is a nasty game that some customers have down very well.

The basic strategy here is don't react or take it personally and don't get engaged with this customer. Simply withdraw, go to someone else, say something like, "Just a second," and pull away. This is very hard to do because bartenders have their own pride and dignity, and believe it looks weak to pull away. Keep in mind that it is the customers who have been drinking, not the bartender. However, bartenders have more power when they pull away and refuse to be drawn in, because the customer is not getting what he or she wants. Moreover, when the bartender returns he or she has the power to follow-up as needed.

Quotable Quote

Don't take it personally when customers get a bit hostile and don't let their problems become your problem. Take care of the situation and let them know in a respectful, yet firm way, that you are in charge.

~James C. Cole, Jr., Bartender~

Continued Attacks on the Bartender

If these attacks continue, the bartender needs to let the customer know that this situation has gone too far. The bottom line is that a bartender does not have to put up with continued abuse. There are two basic steps for managing this situation. First, the bartender must stay away from or ignore this person, do not serve him or her, serve others or be busy with other things. Don't even look at this person. The message is that, "If you want my attention this is not the way to get it." If the abuse continues, then the bartender should deal with the person directly. Here the bartender must be firm, matter of fact and show self-control. Approach the person, use his or her name if you know it and say something like, "Jonesy, this has gone too far, you need to back off or I'll ask you to leave." Then pull away and go to another customer. If the person backs off and settles down, the bartender should return to see if anything is needed. While these customers may have backed off and become more subdued, the bartender must realize that they are still angry, though quiet, and can easily flare up again if provoked. If the customer continues to be abusive, then the bartender should follow through and ask the customer to leave.

Confrontational Person Returns on Another Day

It is common enough that a customer was confrontational one day with another customer or the bartender and was asked to leave and then returns on another day. In these situations the bartender should give this person a fresh start. Keep in mind that the person was asked to leave, but was not told to stay away.

It is possible that the offending person may be feeling pretty sheepish about what happened and will need to save face a little. The bartender can help here by just accepting the person as a regular customer and basically communicating business as usual.

However, if this customer starts up again with the same confrontational behavior such as loud arguing or throwing around insults, the bartender needs to act quickly by telling the person, "Look Jonesy, here we go again. You need to back off, or you are out for good." Keep in mind too, that the other customers don't want this kind of behavior in the bar, and they expect you to take care of the problem. If you don't, more than likely you will lose their respect and they may drift to another bar.

Refusing to Serve More Drinks

Some customers, when they reach these upper levels of 7 through 8, show signs that they have had too much to drink and should not be served more alcohol. At this stage, bartenders must let the customers know that they cannot be served any more alcohol. While it is a judgment call, it is an important part of a bartenders' responsibility to deny a customer further drinks if in their judgment, the customer has consumed sufficient or too much alcohol. Typically, bartenders receive information and training on how to recognize these signs and how to refuse additional drinks to customers as part of their licensing program.

A very common strategy is to let customers know ahead of time that they have reached their limit. For example, a bartender may say, "Joe. Look we need to make this your last drink. OK. I can't have you over the top." Another bartender may offer a non-alcoholic drink with a comment like, "Hey Sarah, I can't serve you any more alcohol. Can I get you a coffee or a soft drink?"

It is important for bartenders to remember that they don't have to convince customers that they have had enough to drink; otherwise you will get into a useless argument. Simply stay with the statement that you cannot serve any more drinks if in your judgment the customer has had enough alcohol.

It is also very important to try to let customers know that you are looking out for their best interests and safety versus being the bad guy and having to punish them. It is just like a coach who takes an injured player off the field to rest. The player may strongly wish to keep playing, but the coach knows the player needs to be rested otherwise more serious injuries may happen. In other words, the coach is not punishing the player, rather the coach is showing concern for the player's well being and future. In the bartenders' case, they must follow through with refusing more drinks, but do it in a way that communicates they don't want the customer to get into trouble and that they want the customer to return soon.

When customers who have been refused further alcohol are leaving, it is important to ask them if they have a ride home or if they need a taxi. This is not only a safety measure but also communicates to the customer, and others, that you are looking out for their well-being.

• • • • • • ONLY IN THE BARS • • • • • • • •

A fellow came into a bar and ordered a martini. Before drinking it, he removed the olive and carefully put it into a glass jar. Then he ordered another martini and did the same thing. After an hour the jar was full of olives, he staggered out. "Well," said a customer, "I never saw anything as weird as that!" "Not really," the bartender said. "His wife asked him to pick up a jar of olives on his way home."

Summary of Strategies

Box 4.1:Defusing Beginning Problems
People Skill Guidelines for Bartenders

1. Frequently look around, move around, notice what is happening and be alert.

2. Anticipate problems and act accordingly.

3. Don't let customers take over the bar.

4. Spot the signs of trouble early.

5. Make yourself present in the trouble spot.

6. Approach the problems calmly and respectfully.

7. Provide minor distractions to run interference.

8. Know exactly what known customers do when they are losing it.

9. Use signals or cues with known customers.

10. Be straightforward when giving directions.

11. When customers are confronting each other, move to the situation, make yourself visible and tell them to settle down or they will have to leave.

12. When customers take the role of stirring or inciting problems, move quickly toward them and make your presence felt. Tell them directly to stay out of the problem. If they persist in troublemaking, they should be asked to leave.

13. If the customer confronts the bartender, do not overreact or become engaged. Simply walk away, attend to other customers and return later.

14. When abuse continues, tell the person to stop or he or she will have to leave.

15. When customers return from being sent away, give them a fresh start. But if they start up again, tell them directly to settle down or they will be axed.

16. Refuse serving more alcohol to customers who show signs that they have reached their limit. Notify them ahead of time that this is their last drink or offer the option of a non-alcoholic drink. Be sure to check that these customers have a ride home or offer to call a taxi.

Chapter Summary

Some customers, after several drinks, may show the signs of beginning problems. It is a very important for bartenders to anticipate these changes so that the situations can be defused; otherwise, the bar can become tense and a serious incident may occur.

Usually, there are signs of unrest in a bar to indicate that problems may arise. These are signs of tension and usually can be spotted by the bartender. In these situations, the bartender must act quickly but not abruptly. The key is to approach the trouble spot in a calm, respectful, and measured manner so that the problem can be nipped in the bud.

If there is hostility between customers, bartenders must try to defuse the situation by approaching the customers fairly quickly, and doing what they can to be very visible to the involved customers, such as by checking to see if anything is needed. If the confrontation continues, the bartender must ask the customers to settle down or they will be refused service. It is better to stop serving them at this point, than to wait for a serious incident and then be forced to ask them to leave.

Similar strategies are used if the customer becomes confrontational with the bartender. First and foremost, bartenders must not overreact and become engaged or combative with the customer. If they do, things will only worsen. Bartenders should pull away, and go to other customers or get busy somewhere else. If the hostilities persist, then the bartender needs to draw a line and tell the person that this needs to stop or he or she will have to leave.

ONLY IN THE BARS

A termite crawls into a bar and asks, "Where is the bar tender?"

5

Dealing with Serious Behavior

Diagram 5.1: Serious Problems, Levels 9-10

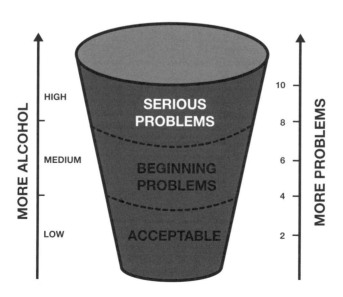

Well, this is the worst case scenario in a bar. Diagram 5.1: Serious Problems, Levels 9-10, shows customers escalating to serious problem behavior. The glass is full now showing levels 9 through 10. Here the customers become violent and unsafe. Fortunately, it is something that happens very rarely and perhaps never in some bars. However, there is always the chance that certain customers, after they have been drinking, may become violent and attack other customers or make the bar unsafe. For these reasons, the topic is addressed in this chapter.

As with the previous levels, it is not uncommon for this customer to begin drinking at the acceptable level of behavior. However, with continued drinking and perhaps negative exchanges with other customers, this customer progresses to the highest levels of serious behavior (Levels 9-10).

It is important to realize that this progression in levels of behavior from acceptable, to beginning problems to serious problems can happen very fast, where the stages become blurred. Also, other unknown factors may come into play, such as the customer may already have been drinking, using drugs, or carrying a grudge against someone else and is looking for a fight. Regardless, there are things the bartender can do to prevent the customer from reaching these levels (these strategies are described in Chapters 3 and 4). Often, in hind sight, the bartender or owner probably should have evicted the customer before reaching this stage. The bottom line is that other customers do not come to a bar to witness serious behavior, fights, assaults, serious injury or a fatality. Customers demand and expect a safe environment. Consequently, bartenders must take every step possible to prevent serious problems. However, if a customer does

Serious Problems in the Bar

"Say that again you..."

"C'mon. Cool it!"

show serious problems, then there are safety procedures the bartender must follow which are described in this chapter.

Main Aim
Follow Emergency Procedures Swiftly To Ensure Safety For All

Customers come to a bar for a few drinks with friends or to relax by themselves in a comfortable environment. If a customer or customers reach a level where violence may occur or already has occurred, the bartender must move quickly and follow the emergency procedures established for this bar. The bottom line is safety for all. Most customers will not come to a bar where violence happens frequently or is managed poorly. They expect to be in a safe place.

What You See
Serious Problems: Levels 9-10

Now we are dealing with the worst case scenario- violent behavior or a major incident. At this point a fight may be happening, the noise level has escalated, furniture or equipment may be damaged and people may get hurt- not only those involved, but also the bystanders.

Level 9

The things you are likely to see at this level can be categorized as physical, which include:
- Throwing furniture around the bar
- Breaking glasses
- Sweeping glasses and other table items onto the floor
- Loud, with in-your-face shouting and swearing
- Customers suddenly getting to their feet and squaring off
- Pushing, shoving and hitting
- Fighting
- Brawling
- Other signs you might notice

Level 10

This level is the top of the scale and is the most serious because the intent of the customer is to cause harm to another customer. The signs at Level 10 are:
- Any of the behavior listed above for Level 9
- Pulling and using a weapon (gun or knife)
- Using bar items as weapons (such as a broken glass or bottle, cue stick, billiard ball, or furniture item)
- Other signs you might notice

· · · · · · ONLY IN THE BARS · · · · · · · · ·

A grasshopper went into a bar and the bartender said, "You know we have a drink named after you." The grasshopper says, "So you have a drink named Mike?"

What You Do: Levels 9-10
Strategies for Dealing with Serious Problems

It is absolutely essential for bartenders to know the bar's procedures to follow when problems reach this level. The situation must be managed swiftly to prevent injury and damage to property. Customers need to feel safe in a bar, otherwise they will not come back; the bar will get a bad reputation that ends up hurting the business. There are also liability issues if the incidents are not managed properly.

Defuse the Situation if Possible

The first and strongest suggestion is for bartenders to routinely follow the guidelines and strategies described in the previous two chapters (Chapters 3 and 4 respectively). The idea is that if the bartender is alert, keeping an eye on the customers, noticing the beginnings of problems and acting swiftly to defuse the situations, then the customer most likely will not get to the serious problem levels. However, on rare occasions, the situation will escalate and the bartender may not have to opportunity to nip the problem in the bud. In these cases, the bar's emergency procedures must be followed.

Know the Bar's Emergency Procedures

When violent behavior occurs, bartenders should never be in a position of wondering what should be done. The procedures should be automatic. Every bartender must know exactly what to do in these situations and owners or managers must make it their business to carefully inform and train their personnel in the procedures. Bartenders should never have to "fly by the seat of their pants," in these serious situations. The steps to be followed should be black and white.

Know the Options

There are a variety of procedures to be followed when there is a major incident. Some of the options include calling in security, making a police call, or using bouncers. In some cases the owners or managers demand to be called immediately. Most times, the bartender is required to write a brief report to document the incident for follow-up and in case charges are pressed. Again, whatever options are used comes down to what the owner or manager requires.

Keep as Calm as Possible

Even though a serious situation can be very worrying or nerve-wracking, bartenders must remain calm and in control of themselves. If they get emotional then they are less likely to follow the procedures and will likely make mistakes and escalate the situation. Moreover, if they lose control of their own emotions they will probably forget some important details or the details may become blurred. The bartender's role is to remain calm and follow the procedures in a matter-of-fact, deliberate and efficient manner.

It is interesting to watch the old time westerns when a brawl breaks out with gunshots fired into the ceilings, windows smashed, chairs and tables broken, and bodies flying everywhere. Of special interest is the demeanor of the bartender. They are always calm, detached and to some extent, try to maintain service. Not that we want to see that level of violence in the bars today, but the deportment of these western bartenders is very consistent with what we are recommending in this book.

Remove Offending Customers

The usual practice for dealing with out-of-control customers, who are involved in a fight, brawl, or throwing things around, is to remove them from the bar. The bartender simply says something like, "Look you need to leave the bar now," and persists with this message. Don't be in a big hurry to get them out of the bar by pushing them or grabbing and tugging on their arms because they may escalate or turn on you. Stay with the message that they need to leave, repeating the words and pointing to the door. Keep in mind that customers at this level of behavior are not very rational and that their judgment is impaired. They are fired up because of the fight or incident and usually have had too much to drink. So the simpler and more direct the message to leave the bar, the better. If they refuse to leave after a few efforts to get them to leave, bartenders usually are expected to call for backup: security, the owner or manager or the police. The manager or owner should have these procedures tied down for the bartender to follow.

Avoid Being Combative

Even though the customer's behavior is offensive and has no place in the bar, it is most important that the bartender avoid becoming combative, such as by getting in the customer's face, shouting at the customer, or becoming physically threatening. The reason is that when the bartender gets involved like this, the customers may escalate or turn on the bartender, leading to fighting or brawling with the bartender. The enraged customer will interpret this exchange as, "So you wanna fight too?" The strong recommendation is to stay as calm as possible, be firm and matter-of–fact, avoid being combative and follow the procedures.

Use of Force

This is always a very tricky issue. How far should bartenders go in breaking up a fight or removing customers? Clearly, once bartenders get involved physically, they may get hurt or even worsen the situation. Other customers may join in as well to defend the bartender or their buddies, resulting in a free-for-all brawl. One obvious issue is that for force to be effective, the bartender has to be stronger than the involved customer. Sometimes, this is not the case. So if some bartenders can use force and others cannot, then there are problems of consistency with procedures. It is best to have one procedure for all staff to follow.

If force has to be used, it is best to utilize people who are trained in these procedures such as security or the police. Generally, bartenders are told not to use force, and if they are expected to use force, then they should be fully trained in safe procedures and be physically capable of using the procedures effectively.

In addition, sometimes it is advisable to use force defensively. Again, training is needed for these defensive techniques.

If the customer, showing serious problem behavior, is with some friends, sometimes the bartender can call upon the friends to help out. Again, it is not the bartender versus the customer. Rather, the bartender is calling upon the customer's friends to assist in having the customer leave. The customer will probably listen to the friends or go along with them. This strategy is more likely to be successful if the bartender already has the friends' respect.

Keep Good Documentation

It is most important for the bartender to carefully observe what is going on in a major incident. The bartender should note all involved persons and any particular actions. For example, if a chair gets thrown and a window broken, the bartender should note who threw the chair and what damage was done. Also, bartenders usually note any statements that are made, or more specifically, who said what during the incident. Bartenders should note their own actions, what they did and what they said during the course of the incident. Finally, the bartender should write down these details shortly after the incident is over. It is easy to forget details, so it helps to have things written down as early as possible. This kind of report can be very important too if there are charges or a follow-up investigation, as some customers will deny what happened or tell an entirely different story.

De-Brief and Follow-Up

An important step when a serious incident occurs is to de-brief the situation. That is, the owner or manager and involved staff walk through all that happened from the beginning of the incident to the end. This step is to check to see that the procedures were followed, if the procedures were adequate or if they need adjusting. The intent of de-briefing is not to blame anyone, rather to process what happened and to see if things could have been managed differently if this situation arises again. This step is also very important for bartenders new to the job or with bartenders who may have worked for awhile, but have never before experienced a major incident on their shift.

It is also important to note occasions when problem behavior is more likely to occur. Sometimes it can be predictable, such as following the last home game of the season or during special holidays and events. Also, certain days and times of the week may bring more problems than others. For example, late in the evening on a Friday or Saturday might present more problems than other times. Once the bartenders and owners are aware of the times, days or circumstances when problems are more likely to occur, they can be more alert and try to keep the lid on things.

In addition there may be some decisions regarding follow-up. For example, the incident may have been serious enough that a decision is made, usually by the owner or manager, that one or more of the customers may need to be told that they cannot return to the bar. The bartenders need to have this information in case the customers should return.

Address Repeated Acts of Violent Behavior

Violent behavior in the bar should be a rarity. It should be a red flag if major blow-ups or acts of violent behavior occur very often, such as every other week or even once a month. Emergency procedures must be in place, but if the bartender has to refer to these procedures very often, then something is wrong and needs to be identified. This means that the staff, including the manager or owner, needs to get together to see what is happening and how to prevent these situations from recurring. They need to pinpoint what is going on that permits such unacceptable levels of behavior. Something must be missing in the way the early phases, acceptable and beginning problem levels, are managed. The most common reasons are: the bartender is too slow to respond, which permits things to build up to unacceptable levels; some customers need to be turned away if they are frequently causing these serious problems; and lastly these customers may be having too much to drink and should be refused service earlier. It may be necessary to employ security staff if the violent incidents happen too often especially if there are large crowds in the bar or the bar is in a rough area.

 $\cdots\cdots$ **ONLY IN THE BARS** $\cdots\cdots$

A horse walks into the bar and the bartender says, "Why the long face?"

Summary of Strategies

Box 5.1:Dealing with Serious Problems
People Skill Guidelines for Bartenders

1. Defuse the situation if possible. Use strategies in Chapters 3 and 4.

2. Make sure you know the emergency procedures for when there is a blow-up or major incident.

3. Strictly follow the options required by the owner or manager.

4. Remain calm, show self control and follow the procedures.

5. Avoid being combative. Be calm, firm and matter-of-fact.

6. Do not get involved physically. If you are expected to get involved physically, make sure you are trained in safety procedures. Use defensive measures only as necessary.

7. Pay special attention to details in an incident- involved persons, injuries, damages, what was said and actions taken. Write down these details shortly after the incident is over.

8. Key players (owner or manager) and involved staff should meet to walk through how the situation was managed and make adjustments to the procedures as necessary.

9. Address repeated acts of violent behavior. Find out what may be causing the problems and take measures to correct them.

Quotable Quote

I tell my bartenders that Friday nights and Saturday nights and the night before public holidays, are when they need to be at their best. They have to be on their toes and catch problems early.

~Howell Braun, Bar Owner~

Chapter Summary

Dealing with violent behavior is the worst case scenario for the bartender. These situations can become very ugly, people can get hurt, property damage can occur, regular customers may go somewhere else to avoid these scenes and there could be litigation. The major theme in this book is that most of these situations can be prevented if the bartender is alert, catches problems early and acts quickly to defuse situations.

However, there are times when the bartender cannot nip the problem in the bud, such as with customers who may be using drugs or come in from another bar already fired up and looking for a fight. In these cases, escalation occurs quite quickly and the bartender has to follow the emergency procedures laid out by the owner or manager. Bartenders should not be expected to figure out what to do here. Rather they should strictly follow the directives of the owner or manager. Usually, the involved customers are asked to leave the bar and if they refuse to leave, assistance is called in such as the police or security. In rare cases, bartenders have to take charge of the situation by themselves. In these exceptional cases they need to be carefully trained, especially in defensive procedures with which they can prevent themselves from being hurt in an incident.

It is also very helpful to de-brief the situation to ensure the procedures are followed or whether adjustments need to be made. Good records need to be kept, and if serious incidents occur frequently then the bartenders and manager or owner need to carefully examine what is going on to cause the escalations, and then take measures to correct the problems.

6

Working With a Large Group of Customers

Until now, the focus in this book has been to apply people skills to individual customers or to small groups of customers. However, there is another situation bartenders will find themselves in, and that is the need to work with a large group of customers. For example, a sports team may gather at the bar for an end of the season get together or to celebrate a victorious season; a large group of office workers may gather for a special retirement party for one of their colleagues; or a large group of motorcyclists may drop in on their way home from a gathering somewhere. In some cases a large group may drop in on a regular basis such as a sports team after each game. In general, it is relatively common for a bar to host a large group of customers from time to time.

It is possible that bartenders may become anxious when a large group rolls into the bar because they might think that they cannot serve such a large group, or that things may get out of control. There are several strategies described in the chapter that will help bartenders to be able to serve a large group effectively and at the same time keep the lid on behavior.

The people skills strategies for bartenders described in the previous chapters still apply to working with large groups. The bartenders are still expected to be pleasant and welcoming, provide friendly service, catch problems early and deal with problems that may arise. These practices apply whether you are dealing with one person or a group of twenty or more. The purpose of this chapter is to highlight the differences that a bartender may use to work more effectively with a large group of customers to ensure that these customers have a good time, are taken care of, and that problems are anticipated and defused.

Working with a large group from the office

Plan Ahead for a Good Set-Up When Possible

If the manager or owner of the bar knows in advance that a large group is coming, then the ideal situation is to designate an area of the bar, or a separate room if it is available, for the group. In addition, the owner may assign certain staff to serve the group and other staff to take care of the rest of the bar.

Some owners keep a list of staff who can be called in at short notice to work a few hours, should a large group drop in at the bar. Or, if the owner is not present, the arrangement is for the bartender to call the owner for extra assistance.

When a group drops into the bar without notification, such as a group of players after a game or a group of teachers following a conference day, then the bartender or owner will need to quickly rearrange tables and chairs so the group can sit together if they wish. Promptness in accommodating a large group makes them feel welcome.

Know What to Expect

As you might expect, there are a great variety of large groups that may come to a bar with different needs and expectations. One group may want a relatively quiet get together where they can all see each other and talk to each other, such as a group of teachers following a conference day. Another group, such a motorcyclists, often want some recognition or attention especially in talking about their bikes. A different group, such as a team gathering on the occasion of winning the league championship, is there to party, celebrate and have fun. This group may become quite rowdy, with singing, much laughter, shouting across the room to each other, wanting the music turned up, and may be inclined to drink too much. It is important for bartenders to assess what group they have and especially what particular needs the group might have. In this way the bartender can be more effective in serving them.

Provide Timely Service

One of the biggest challenges in serving large groups is how to get them their drinks in a timely manner. This can be quite intimidating for a bartender. However, there are some steps that can be taken to provide reasonably quick service.

In most cases, the large group ends up breaking up into smaller groups, probably so that they can hear each other talk. The bartender then serves each of these smaller groups in turn making the service much easier to manage and simpler to remember orders.

Another strategy is to keep the drinks as simple as possible. Clearly, 20 people ordering a full range of mixed drinks would be a formidable task for the bartender not only to remember them all, but it would take a long time to mix the drinks. Obviously, the service is quicker and more manageable if the group orders pitchers or jugs of beer, or individual beers and wine. If some in the group insists on having the more complicated drinks to make, then the bartender might say, "Let me get the beer and wine first, and then I'll get the mixed drinks." In this way the simpler drinks are on the table quickly and the mixed drink orders are delayed a little, but do not hold up everyone else.

One owner reported that small groups within a large group typically finish their drinks roughly at the same time. The reason given was a common practice where each person in the group takes a turn to buy a round, so they pace themselves to finish somewhat together. On this basis, bartenders must keep an eye on the group to see when they need to buy a round. In addition, whoever is buying the round will come to the bar for the order which makes it easier for the bartender to serve the group.

Bartenders can also use the groups' practice of finishing their drinks together as an opportunity to collect glasses, pick up as needed and to wipe down the tables.

On the surface a large group can be intimidating, but generally they organize themselves into smaller groups which become the unit for service. Bartenders serve one small group then move onto the next and so on.

Quicken the Pace of Service

Clearly, a large group puts more demands on the bartender's time and makes it more difficult to serve all customers quickly. Assigning staff to the group is the ideal way to ensure quality service to the group and to the rest of the customers. However, sometimes additional staff is not immediately available. In these cases the bartender must make adjustments. Basically they need to put on their "runners." That is, they have to change the pace of how they serve customers such as by walking more quickly along the bar or to the tables, pouring the drinks faster and having less conversation time with the customers. In other words, bartenders do what they can to save time and quicken their service.

Clean Tables More Often

If two customers are drinking together and there are a couple of empty glasses on the table, it is not really a problem. However, if a large group of twenty customers is gathered around some tables and there is an empty glass or two per customer, then we could be looking at 30-40 glasses on the tables, which would look cluttered and untidy. The bartender must make an extra effort to keep the tables clear of empty glasses and bottles and to wipe the tables down as frequently as possible. Again, the message is that bartenders needs to, "Put on their 'runners,'" when it comes to keeping the tables clean and providing timely service.

Connect with the Regulars

Sometimes the regulars in the bar become resentful and complain when there is a large group in the bar. The reason is obvious. The level of service cannot be the same as it would be if the large group was not there, and with most large groups the noise level is considerably raised, which can annoy the regulars. It is very important for the bartender to try to provide good service to the regulars when a large group is present. But the bottom line is that the bar is different when a large group is present, and there is not much the bartender can do about it. When a regular complains, all the bartender can say is something like, "It's tough getting around to everyone. I'm doing my best." Generally, the regular just wants to complain and knows full well that the presence of a large group changes things.

It is sometimes helpful to "inflate the ego" of the regular with a comment like, "Look Joe, you are one of our regulars, which we appreciate." In some cases, because the group is so large and staff to serve them is not really enough, some bartenders offer the regular a free drink with a comment like, "Sorry for being so slow to get to you. This large crowd is overwhelming us. How about having a free beer on me?"

Keep an Eye on Supplies

When there is a large group present or even two large groups, there is a good chance that essential supplies may run out. For example, if bartenders are not careful and plan as they go, they may run out of clean glasses, ice, or liquor such as bourbon. Also be sure that sufficient kegs are connected so that service is not interrupted while new kegs are being connected.

Managing Beginning Problems

There is always a chance that some of the group may begin to show problems when a large group gathers, especially when the group is celebrating something. The same strategies suggested in Chapter 4 for anticipating and defusing problems apply. There is one additional tool that can be quite effective with large groups, and that is to enlist support from the other members of the group. For example, if one member of the group is on his feet shouting and swearing, or trying to dance on the table, the bartender might approach other members near this person, or approach an obvious leader if there is one, and ask them something like, "Can you get your buddy to tone it down?" Or, "He is going too far, can you get him to settle down?" Or the bartender might tell the other members that "Your friend here will be refused further drinks if he can't settle down." Group members typically do not want trouble. They realize that they may be excluded from bar in the future if the situation is not brought under control. In effect, the other group members can be a very strong ally to the bartender if some members start to become a problem.

Again, it is very important to monitor the group's alcohol consumption and keep an eye on its behavior. It may be necessary to pull the plug and let the group know that no further alcohol will be served if their behavior warrants this decision.

Sometimes it is difficult for the bartender to know how much an individual in a large group may be drinking. For example, the group may be ordering large pitchers of beer and one member drinks more glasses than another, which cannot be tracked by the bartender. However, the bartender needs to be on the alert and watch the member's behavior. If there are signs of beginning problems, then the bartender needs to act accordingly (as described in Chapter 4).

Deal with Serious Problems

Hopefully, serious problems or incidents will not occur, but if they do then bartenders need to act swiftly, perhaps more so than with isolated small groups of customers. The reason is that with a larger crowd, more customers may become involved. So instead of a bar room fight, there might be a free-for-all brawl or melee. Again, the bartender should enlist the support of the group members who are behaving appropriately to settle the others down, or simply say it is time to leave. Otherwise, the bartender should follow the normal emergency procedures described in Chapter 5.

Use Security Staff When Close Supervision is Necessary

Most bars can handle the ebb and flow of customer crowds, with good management, quality service and effective people skills by owners, managers and bartenders. However, there are definite occasions when security staff needs to be employed. The reason is that the regular staff cannot provide the undivided level of supervision needed for these occasions because their attention is also taken up with serving customers. Security staff typically has the sole responsibility of crowd control with screening customers, active supervision and especially in preventing and managing customer conflicts or problems.

Security staff is usually employed to help with crowd control in bars where there are large gatherings of customers. These venues include late night discos and night clubs, busy seasonal bars, those bars that consistently attract large crowds. Also security staff is often used in smaller bars in neighborhoods where there may be more fights or problems and where the screening and supervision of incoming customers is critical.

We argue that security staff should also be well trained in the areas outlined in this book for catching problems early, using sound defusion strategies, and for managing the more serious problems using safe procedures especially if force has to be applied.

Summary of Strategies

The strategies recommended for bartenders to follow in working with a large group of customers are summarized in Box 6.1.

Box 6.1:Working With a Large Group of Customers
People Skill Guidelines for Bartenders
1. Plan ahead for a good set-up when possible.
2. In general use the people skills described in previous chapters for individual or small groups of customers.
3. Know what to expect with the particular group.
4. Provide timely service.
5. Quicken the pace of service.
6. Clean tables more often.
7. Manage orders in smaller groups.
8. Connect with regulars as best as possible.
9. Keep an eye on essential supplies.
10. Manage beginning problems quickly.
11. Use group members to help control members who may be causing problems.
12. Deal with serious problems quickly.
13. Use security staff when close supervision is necessary.

Chapter Summary

There is every chance that bartenders at some point, will be expected to work with a large group of customers. It is important for the bartender to have a sense of what the large group is there for and what the group needs or expects. One group might be there to celebrate and have a fun evening. Another group might be there to get together, enjoy each other's company, keep to themselves and have a nice quiet afternoon. The bartender should determine the different needs that large groups have to better serve them.

Perhaps the biggest impact that large groups have on the bar is in the area of service. More customers obviously put bigger demands on the bartender, especially when it comes to timely service. Typically, large groups sort themselves out into smaller groups so the bartenders need to recognize these sub-groups and work with them in turn. It is better to serve the simpler drinks such as beer and wine first, and the more time consuming drinks, mixed drinks, last. The bartender has to make adjustments to quicken the time it takes to serve people. It is also important to keep an eye on regular supplies in the bar, because with larger numbers there is more chance that supplies will be depleted. When some of the members in a group show beginning problems, one of the key strategies is to lean on other members of the group to help take care of the problem. The individual showing the problems is more likely to listen to other members of the group than the bartender. In addition, the group does not want to get a bad name or be embarrassed by one of their own members. Otherwise, bartenders should use the people skills described in the earlier chapters when they are working with large groups of customers.

 Quotable Quote

I love the challenge of a big group, because it keeps me busy and I have more fun.

~Tiffany Esperago, Bartender~

7

Putting it All Together

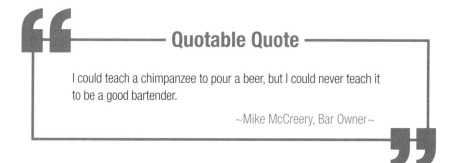

Quotable Quote

I could teach a chimpanzee to pour a beer, but I could never teach it to be a good bartender.

~Mike McCreery, Bar Owner~

The point in this statement, from a successful bar-owner, is that there is much more to being a bartender than serving drinks. This book is written to provide assistance to bartenders on a very important aspect of what this "much more" involves. That is, the effective use of good people skills.

There is no question that bartenders have a very challenging job. As well as having many things to do in the course of their work, their biggest challenge is having to do many of these jobs at the same time. They have to be very skilled at multi-tasking. One very important part of this multi-tasking is using good people skills and that is:

- knowing how to get along with people,
- ensuring that customers are made welcome and are treated well,
- being able to anticipate problems,
- using tact at the right time,
- knowing how to calm things down,
- being able to defuse conflicts,
- following emergency procedures as needed.

It is most important for the bartender to understand the connection between the customers' behavior and consumption of alcohol. The basic understanding is that the more customers drink, the more likely there will be changes in their behavior and in a loss of self-control and good judgment.

Making a Difference

It is hoped that as bartenders work through the pages in this book, they will come to realize that, yes, they can make a huge difference in their bar's atmosphere. To make this point, in Box 7.1 two bars are described, Smithies Pub and The Barrel.

"OK. It's a bet..."

Box 7.1: Story of Two Bars	
Smithies Pub	**The Barrel**
When you walk into this bar, here is what you see. It is very noisy. The juke-box is roaring, and customers are shouting at each other. Most tables are littered with dirty glasses and there are spillages on the floor. A few chairs are turned over on the floor. The bartender is standing behind the bar looking very serious, with his head down, and hurrying to serve drinks. A few customers are also standing at the bar, shouting at the bartender to get them a drink quickly. Profanities can be heard all over the bar. Two customers in the corner of the bar are trading insults and squaring off while three others are standing there egging them on. You could feel the tension in the bar. The restroom is dirty and smelly. The carpet is ripped and covered with stains. One customer mentioned that if you think this is bad, come here on Friday or Saturday nights then you'll see some real action. There have been fights here each weekend over the past few weeks. Many regulars have left and gone to other places. Several of the customers have been axed from other bars. The owner won't do anything, as he thinks this is the way it has to be when people drink. There has been a big turnover in staff resulting in new bartenders here every other week.	When you walk into this bar, here is what you see. The juke-box is on but not too loud. Customers are sitting around chatting, a couple have their heads in newspapers, a few are watching a game on TV, several are sitting at the bar talking among themselves and to the bartender. The bartender moves to the tables collecting empty glasses and bottles, wipes down the table tops and pushes in chairs. While she does this she nods to some customers coming in and waves to two who are leaving. She heads back to the bar and pours some more drinks, chats to the customers who ordered the drinks, smiles at the newcomers and signals she will be with them in a second. The restrooms are clean. The carpets are also clean without stains or tears. When you listen hard you cannot hear any profanities and certainly there is no one shouting or in anyone's face. The bar has a very relaxed tone and the customers look like they are enjoying themselves. The bartender, although busy, looks very comfortable and appears to be enjoying the passing contact with all the customers. She has been working at this bar for three years now and there has been was very little turnover in staff.

If you asked any bartender, "Where would you prefer to work: Smithies or at The Barrel?" the answer would be obvious, The Barrel. However, it would be a mistake to say that the owner and staff at The Barrel were lucky to draw the customers they have and that Smithies was unlucky to have what they have. The authors of this book would be willing to put a wager that if the owner and the staff from The Barrel were to take over Smithies, that in a reasonably short time Smithies would be transformed. The reason is that the atmosphere in a bar is controlled by an owner or manager with good management skills and bartenders with good service and people skills. Moreover, once Smithies Pub was brought under control, the bartenders, by using their people skills, would be able to maintain the nice, positive atmosphere described for The Barrel in Box 7.1, and also prevent problems from occurring.

A major message in this book is that the bartender, with support from the owner or manager, can make a huge difference in the atmosphere of a bar. They can establish the kind of bar they want to have.

Note: It is understood that the bartender is competent in mixing drinks, knows the laws governing drinking in public places and can deliver drinks in a reasonable amount of time. People skills are not a substitute for these basic competencies. Rather, the key message in this book is that bartenders who have the basic competencies and have good people skills, are in a strong position to establish and control the atmosphere of a bar.

Preventing Problems and Eliminating Serious Problems

In Chapter 2, the customers' behavior in a bar was described in terms of a triangle with the base of the triangle representing the low end of behavior on a scale of one through ten. This behavior was considered to be acceptable. The middle section of the triangle referred to the customers who were showing beginning problems. The top part of the triangle, represented customers showing the most serious behavior. The theme of this book is that if the bartenders pay attention to what is going on at the lower levels and act in a timely manner when customers show the beginnings of problem behavior, problems of the upper levels will be prevented. This means that the scale of behavior shown by the customers would now fall in the range of levels one through five or six (as would be the case for The Barrel described in Box 7.1). Levels seven through ten would be prevented and the bartender would not have to deal with these upper levels of behavior.

In looking at the diagrams presented in Chapter 2, the customer levels of behavior would not go beyond Level 6 (see Figure 7.1) and the triangle would have the top portion removed, Levels 7-10 (see Figure 7.2).

Diagram 7.1: Levels of Customer Behavior with Competent Bartender

(Note: The upper levels on the scale, Levels 7-10, have been eliminated.)

Note: Of course, the exception would be where some customers may come in off the street already wound up and looking for trouble. In these cases the standard emergency procedures should be quickly followed.

Diagram 7.2: Spread of Customer Behavior in a Well Run Bar

(Note: The top part of the triangle representing the most serious problem behaviors, Levels 7-10, is eliminated.)

BEGINNING PROBLEMS
(Levels 5-8)
Some: Occasionally

ACCEPTABLE BEHAVIOR
(Levels 1-4)
The Vast Majority: Most of the Time

It is most important for bartenders to realize that they are in charge of the bar and can control its atmosphere. To accomplish this, they must be very alert and use defusion skills at the very beginnings of problem behavior, Levels 5 and 6, to prevent further problems.

However, even if the bartender is very good, and there is strong support from the owner or manager, problems may arise simply because customers can walk in off the street and cause problems so that levels beyond Level 6 are reached. In these hopefully rare cases, the bar has a system for dealing with these situations very swiftly (described in Chapters 4 and 5).

In general, the message in this book is for bartenders to pay special attention to four main skills:

1. Provide good, friendly, and timely service.
2. Keep a constant eye on the entire bar.
3. Anticipate problems and act accordingly.
4. Act on what you see in a timely manner to defuse situations.

It is hoped that bartenders who use the information in this book will be more effective and efficient in their work, enjoy their jobs more, become more appreciated by the customers, have a satisfying career in the bar business and become highly valued and successful employees.

Best wishes,
Geoff Colvin
Peter Battistella

Another round please.

Final Thoughts
The following sonnet was written for bar owners, but it could easily serve as a summary statement for the role of bartenders.

WHAT EVERY OWNER (AND BARTENDER) SHOULD HAVE

The humor of Bob Hope

The judgment of Solomon

The racing knowledge of Joe Brown (legendary Australian race caller)

The smile of a film star

The sporting ability of Don Bradman or Babe Ruth

The business acumen of Henry Ford

The punch of Joe Louis

The capacity of a reservoir

The memory of an elephant

The patience of a meander river fisherman

The dignity of an archbishop

The tact of a schoolmaster

The gall of a politician

The voice of a sergeant-major

And last, but not least -------- The hide of a rhinoceros

~Source Unknown~

Credits

This page constitutes an extension of the copyright page. Every effort has been made to trace the ownership of the copyrighted material and to secure permission from copyright holders. In the event of any issue regarding the use of material in this book, we will be pleased to make any corrections in future printings.

Photographs

Credits are due to the following people for participating as subjects for many of the photos in this book: Diana Aguilar, Marc Bloch, Todd Brownson, Melissa Butterfield, Karen Cheang, Garrett Conn, Mark Cumer, Brad Dean, Lee Gaudette, Terry Hall, Jay Hamlin, Darren Hare, Fiona Hogarth, Tim Hogarth, Jose Jaimes, Roger & Nancy Jensen, Sean Lee, Mike Maahs, Daniel Miller, Zachary Miller, Ahren Osterbrink, Jodi Parmer, Jason Powell Anthony Reyes, Sahlia Spaan, Demetrius Spates, Lindsey Spates, Randy Sperl, Trent Thompson, and Mike Wing.

Credits are also due to Getty Creative Images, www.gettyimages.com, for the use of their royalty-free photos.

"Anything else?"